At His Feet

Copyright © 2018 by Angela Stress

At His Feet

From Devastation to Restoration

by Angela Stress

Printed in the United States of America

ISBN-13: 978-1986125598

ISBN-10: 1986125599

All rights reserved solely by the author. The author guarantees all contents are original and do not infringe upon the legal rights of any other person or work. No part of this book may be reproduced in any form without the permission of the author. The views expressed in this book are not necessarily those of the publisher.

Unless otherwise indicated, Bible quotations are taken from The King James Version, American Standard Version; The New King James Version ®. Copyright © 1982 by Thomas Nelson, Inc.; The New International Version, Copyright © 1973, 1978, 1984, 2011 by Biblica, Inc; and The New Living Translation. Copyright © 1996, 2004, 2007 by Tyndale House Foundation.

At His Feet

At His Feet

I dedicate this book to all those who have encouraged me to be all that I can be **IN CHRIST**.

First, to my husband Eddie who has loved me and helped me through every trial I faced in writing this book. He has cried with me, rejoiced with me and even pushed me to continue when I wanted to quit. Honey, I love you more than words can say.

Second, to all of the Godly men and women my Father has placed in my life. To the ministers who taught and encouraged me, I am who I am today because you helped me see who God has called me to be. I thank you all for your service to the Kingdom.

Finally, to prison ministers everywhere. You will never realize until you enter the gates of heaven just how much your labors of love have accomplished. Keep bringing Liberty to the captives!

At His Feet

Forward

Born and raised in Southern West Virginia, Angela Mullins Stress is a remarkable woman of God with a story that transcends social and geographic borders. She is a testament of what redemption can truly do in the life of any person who finds himself or herself in the direst of circumstances. In a world where many believe that there is no such thing as rehabilitation in the prison system, Angela rises and shines as an example of hope through Jesus Christ. She's a reminder to us all that, within the confines of prison walls is an entire mission field. It's an opportunity to turn ashes into beauty. It's an opportunity to bless someone who's perhaps never had a good life, with latter years which make up for the disappointments and mistakes of the former.

I have come to know and love this young woman, and to see a maturity in her that many lifelong Christians never seek to reach. Her hunger for holiness, truth, and close fellowship with her Savior have taken her into depths of the Christian walk at an accelerated rate. To see her operating in the power of God, to hear her teach and preach deep messages of faith, and to pastor and shepherd others with great passion and urgency, it's a joy which never ceases to bless me. What a message: someone lost, addicted, incarcerated, in trouble, and hopeless finds Jesus Christ in the time of her greatest

need. . .becoming convert, student of the Word, Pastor, mother, wife,

and example to all who feel they're too far gone to change.

Angela is formerly the pastor of Redemption House in War, West

Virginia, and has been involved tirelessly in helping the poor and disadvantaged

in her area.   She hosts numerous revivals and outreaches

throughout the year, and is a spiritual mother to many whom she's

won to Christ.   Recently, she had the opportunity to share her story

in a correction facility in Texas, when she was invited to accompany

Mike Barber ministries on this evangelism effort. This book is hopefully

just her first. . .because God's done such a transformation in

her life, surely a few pages can't hold it all!

Lisa Crum, Administrative Assistant and freelance writer;

Regional Church of God; Delbarton W.V.

At His Feet

Endorsements

"In the days of attenders, God has raised up a contender! Angela is the modern day Mary Magdalene, championing the message of mercy, found only at the feet of Jesus."

Colleen Addair,   Radio Personality; WIVK Radio; Knoxville, Tennessee

"Angela is a shining example of the power of Righteousness. Moved only by her love of a Merciful Savior and trusting in His Word, she allowed God to give us a present day example of His mercy, grace and power."

Reverend Judy Logan, Founder, Ladies of Light Ministries; Chapmanville, West Virginia

"Angela was always a special person to me and all the Jail ministers. It wasn't that she had any advantage it was her hunger that propelled her into all of our hearts. She soaked up the word as if it were life or death. In reality the word is life to all of us who finds it. She has always had the kindest heart toward the addicted and hurting. This book is a testament of her journey from the ashes to the beauty of restoration. She has done it all being at his feet. . This is just the beginning of the Great things the Lord has called her to do. Let Angela show you how to take the words of the Master, apply it to yourself personally, and rise above. Get back what the enemy has stolen from you. What she has done is available to us all."

Tammy Sheppard, Evangelist, Logan, West Virginia

"Words cannot explain how proud and honored I am to write this about someone who I have seen God use in a mighty way. Our stories are similar to the point where I know that God is a healer and he restores anyone who lifts their hand and surrenders. My friend this book of your journey will lead people to a new understanding of surrendering – not in defeat but in victory that Christ gives us in him. Your life your journey your faith will resound the nations. From small coal camps to metropolitan areas. That is just how big and mighty our God is. Thank you for letting Him use you in all your endeavors and thank you for not giving up. This is just the beginning of your chapter and it's EPIC.

Pastor Johnathan Frazier (JFraze—Beech St. Records National Recording Artist), Revolution Tabernacle, Princeton, West Virginia

Introduction

This book is a love story of two women and their King. It's a story of deliverance and redemption.

The woman you may be most familiar with in this story is Mary Magdalene. Jesus said that wherever the gospel was preached her story would be told. The other woman is the story you have probably never heard of: Angela.

Yes, the other woman in the story is none other than myself. You are about to take a journey into both Mary's life and my life to see how our King took us from a horrible past and provided us a brand new life. Jesus Christ gave us both beauty for ashes.

At His Feet

Chapter 1

A Rough Start

I was a troubled child who came from a broken home. My parents divorced when I was 10 years old. This led me into a life of emotional turmoil and constant fear. I looked for love and acceptance wherever I could find it. I tried the local churches, and when those churches hurt me I found temporary satisfaction at the local bars. I did everything I knew to dull the pain and stop the heartache I felt inside. I tried drinking, men and drugs; still nothing ever filled the void I felt in my heart. I was running from one man to the next and from one broken relationship to another.

I found myself at the feet of a man who would change my life forever.

Mary was a woman who had lived a broken life. She was raised in a city where religion was the top of everyone's priority list. However, love was the last priority on that list. Her attempt to find love resulted instead in a life of sin. One compromise at a time, one broken heart after another, Mary lost her self-worth. Instead of just giving herself away, she felt she might as well profit from the shame of her life, selling herself as a prostitute. In a town full of religion, Mary found no one to love her and no one to help her.

Mary was hurt by the religious leaders of her time and found

At His Feet

herself at the feet of a man who would take the broken pieces of her life and make something wonderful of them.

I find it strange how two women born 2,000 years apart could have so much in common. It's phenomenal how the very same man could capture both our hearts and turn our lives around.

Let me tell you our stories, and take you through all of the times both Mary and I have found ourselves at His feet. . .

At His Feet

Chapter 2

The Sinful Woman

John 8:1-8 (KJV)

8 Jesus went unto the mount of Olives.

2And early in the morning he came again into the temple, and all the people came unto him; and he sat down, and taught them.

3And the scribes and Pharisees brought unto him a woman taken in adultery; and when they had set her in the midst,

4 They say unto him, Master, this woman was taken in adultery, in the very act.

5Now Moses in the law commanded us, that such should be stoned: but what sayest thou?

6 This they said, tempting him, that they might have to accuse him. But Jesus stooped down, and with his finger wrote on the ground, as though he heard them not.

7 So when they continued asking him, he lifted up himself, and said unto them, He that is without sin among you, let him first cast a stone at her.

8And again he stooped down, and wrote on the ground.

9And they which heard it, being convicted by their own conscience, went out one by one, beginning at the eldest, even unto the last: and Jesus was left alone, and the woman standing in the midst.

10 When Jesus had lifted up himself, and saw none but the woman, he said unto her, Woman, where are those thine accusers? hath no man condemned thee?

At His Feet

11 She said, No man, Lord. And Jesus said unto her,

Neither do I condemn thee: go, and sin no more.

Mary was not a woman of reputable character. She worked as a prostitute and found herself being dragged to the feet of Jesus by those who should have helped her. She was caught in the very act of adultery.

It makes me wonder if she had been set up. Doesn't it take two? Where was the man she had been with? In those days, under the law you were stoned to death for adultery. She was not married so the man who committed the sin with her had to be the married one. Where was he? Why wasn't he going to be put to death? It must have been a set up.

Mary was dragged naked, alone, and thrown at the feet of Jesus. The religious leaders awaited their chance to find a solid accusation, some sort of wrong-doing, to pin upon Jesus. They found just that in this poor, broken woman. Using her as a pawn, they found a way to take out this 'trouble maker' Jesus.

I can see Mary now; beaten, bloody and scared to death. I can see her looking up at this man. She knew he was going to have her put to death, he was a man. In her mind all she could think was how that men did not care about women like her. How that she was nothing to those men and they thought more about stray dogs in the city than they thought of her. How that men were all the same and could not be trusted.

All any man had ever done was use and abuse her. They took

At His Feet

pleasure in her body and threw her away like a piece of trash. She expected that Jesus of Nazareth would be no different.

In her eyes, He was the same as all the other religious jokers she had seen throughout her life. Those who promise to be the voice of God, who promise to lead you to a better life. Those who turn and walk right past you when you really need them. Those who only care about themselves and what they can get from you. He would be the same, she thought, and now He was going to use her to get on the good side of the Pharisees and Sadducees. Yes, this would be the last day of her life.

Or so she thought.

Jesus looked upon this woman with nothing but love and compassion. He saw past her sin and the reason she was dragged to His feet. He heard the cry of her heart instead of the cries of the crowd. The lynch mob was so thirsty for blood, it didn't matter if it came from the prostitute or the Jewish carpenter.

"Stone her! Stone her!" the crowd chanted.

Jesus, however, heard Mary. He heard her cry for help. And that's just what His father had sent Him into this world to do. Ignoring the crowd, Jesus stooped beside Mary and started writing in the sand. The bloodthirsty Sanhedrin were puzzled by His behavior and began to question His actions. What was He doing playing in the sand? Had He lost His mind? Wait, what exactly was He writing? How did He know such personal information about them, all the skeletons in their closets — who had told Him?!

At His Feet

Jesus stood and said, "Okay, he who is without sin here, go ahead and throw the first stone. Go ahead, we're waiting. If you think you do not have sin in your life go right ahead and stone this woman." One stone at a time hit the ground beginning with the oldest man there to the youngest. Jesus has a wonderful way of turning the tables on the enemy. As the scandalized crowd drifted away, Jesus found Himself alone with this frightened, naked woman. He was about to prove to her He was not like any man she had ever met in her life.

Mary wondered what had just happened. She knew that by all rights she should be dead already, or at least in horrific pain. By now she should feel the physical trauma from hundreds of rocks striking her body. She wondered what kind of man, exactly, was this Jesus. Was He for real? Why would He take her side against the leaders of the city? Mary was confused by the events that took place before her eyes.

Everyone else left, leaving Mary alone with the Rabbi standing before her. She gazed into the most beautiful eyes she had ever seen. This man, Jesus, smiled and asked her, "Mary, look around you, where are your accusers? Who do you see here? Is there anyone left who brought you to be stoned, is there even one of them left to condemn you?"

She said, "No one is left my Lord."

She said it — **MY LORD!** She recognized that this man was the Messiah, the savior, the one who would redeem her and Israel.

At His Feet

Jesus smiled again and said," I will not condemn you either. Now go and sin no more."

She couldn't believe it! She had finally found a man who was different from every other man in her life! This man could be trusted. He didn't want anything from her, He wanted only to give instead of take. Instead of death, He gave her life. Instead of throwing her to the mob, He sent the mob away in shame.

What kind of man was this? He had to be the Son of God!

Mary would never forget the first time she found herself

At His feet. . .

Chapter 3

Nowhere But Up

Like Mary, I was not a woman of reputable character the first time I found myself at Jesus' feet. I was a drug addict, just arrested for writing thousands of dollars in forged checks to feed that addiction. Life is what threw me at Jesus' feet.

The stereotypical product of a broken home, a mixed up kid grew up to create an emotional basket case: me. I had turned to men at an early age, searching hard for love but never finding the kind I needed.

Most of the men in my life up to that point had only wanted me for my body. I allowed them to use me so I could feel wanted by someone. Like Mary, those men would then throw me away like a piece of trash.

I always felt dirty and worthless. After one broken marriage and my second marriage heading for divorce, I found myself strung out on Oxycontin. I needed something to dull the pain and hide my guilt. Oxycontin became the love of my life; I would do anything to get it.

At His Feet

I found myself with a $1,000 dollar per day needle habit which controlled my life. I stole, wrote bad checks; whatever it took to get my daily fix. I gave up everything for my new-found lover. I lost my children, what little self-worth I had — everything!

Finally, even the drugs became unsatisfying and the depression grew unbearable. I knew something was missing.

On the run from the law I drifted from state to state, living in the backs of cars and inside abandoned houses. I went for days without eating or bathing. I had lost all hope and thought my life would never get better.

That's when the unthinkable happened. My own cousin (who had been just as guilty in most of my crimes as I was) had turned me into the police. I had looked up to this same woman all my life. She had taken me to church since I was a child. I thought if I could trust anyone, I could trust her.

I soon found I could not trust anyone. Even in church all I found was religion and people telling me what I did wrong. I never felt I could measure up or live like the people in church. I didn't fit into

At His Feet

the mold they wanted me to squeeze into.

At one point I lasted about a year in a church. I was even happy for once in my life. I excitedly told my pastor that I felt the call of God on my life to become a minister. He politely explained to me that not everyone was called to preach. That destroyed something deep inside of me, nearly extinguishing a fire the Holy Spirit lit. Once again, like Mary, the religious leaders I trusted to help me took part in dragging me to the feet of Jesus.

I left the church completely after another incident when I felt the leaders of my church could have given me better counsel. My husband at the time was abusive, had affairs and abandoned me more than once. He even went as far as to have an affair with a 13-year-old child. I was never told that I had biblical grounds for divorce. However, I was told that God hates divorce and I needed to walk in love. The result? I stayed with a man who never loved me. I felt hopeless and lost.

Later, my husband had an operation on his lower back and the doctor prescribed Oxycontin for the pain. Being unsupervised in such close proximity to that medication was too much temptation for me. No one ever taught me how to fight against temptation with the Word of God.

I thought if I was tempted, I may as well go ahead and sin. After all, thinking about sinning was just as bad as sinning, right? So I began my affair with Oxycontin once more; one for a backache, one for a pounding headache... Before I knew it I was in worse shape

At His Feet

than I had ever been before.

Breaking the law and on the run, I was in so deep I had nowhere to look but up.

One night we parked beside of a lake to sleep. I was miserable and couldn't go on living that way any longer. I was tired of the drugs, tired of the lifestyle — I was tired of it all! I just wanted to be free!

I cried out to Jesus that night from the backseat of a stolen car. I asked him to do whatever it took to get me back to him.

Even if it meant putting me in jail to do it.

Three weeks later I found myself in a jail cell, broken and hurting, yet with the strangest sense of peace. I found myself at the feet of Jesus. I cried out to Him that day, giving Him my life. I asked Him to take what was left of me and bring glory to His name.

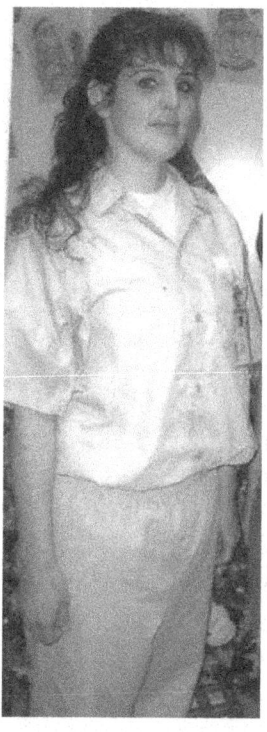

At His Feet

I never really believed I would be anything other than what I was. In my eyes I was a worn out, useless piece of garbage. There at His feet, Jesus saw me differently. Jesus saw the end from the beginning. Like Mary, He saw why I had been created. He knew what He had placed inside of me before the foundation of the world. Jesus didn't see a dirty drug addict. He saw a princess, a child of the King who simply needed to find her true identity in Him.

There I was, giving Jesus my whole heart. This was the end of myself and the end of my past. I was about to fall in love with a man who would turn my entire world as I knew it upside down! This man began teaching me that even though He was all I had, He would be all I ever needed. He didn't care where I came from, what I did in the past. He loved me for me, and in return I loved Him. When someone has been forgiven much, they love much!

He even stopped the death sentence on my life just like He did with Mary. Due to using intravenous drugs, I contracted hepatitis C. The same Jesus who halted the crowd so ready to murder Mary, was beaten so I could be healed of the hepatitis C that surely would have ended my life. What the enemy was going to use to kill me, Jesus turned into a testimony.

Can you see why Mary and I fell in love with this man? He took all our mess and turned it into a message. And He started the very first day we found ourselves **At His feet. . .**

Chapter 4

A New Day

Over the years, I have noticed that most people don't come to Jesus when everything is going right in their lives. For the most part, we find ourselves coming to Him when we have nowhere to look but up.

Maybe you are at the point in your life where you have hit rock bottom; if so this book is for you. God has a wonderful way about Him, He takes those whom the world has given up on and shows off with them. He doesn't think like the world thinks. He doesn't think about us like we think about ourselves.

Jeremiah 29:11 (KJV) For I know the thoughts that I think toward you, saith the Lord, thoughts of peace, and not of evil, to give you an expected end.

God knows the beginning from the end. He knows where we have been and what we have done and He loves us in spite of it all. He wants to take all the hurt, shame and broken dreams of our past and turn it into something beautiful for us. Believe it or not, your sin never took Him by surprise and it does not change the plans He has for your life.

The only one who can stop the future God designed for you is you. No person, no circumstance, no past mistake and not even Satan himself can stop the call of God on your life. Believe me, you do have a call on your life. The only one who has the power to stop it is you.

At His Feet

Jesus came to make all things new. With Mary and myself, He used our past to unlock our purpose. If I had not lived through the things I did, I would not have a heart to do what I am doing now. He will do the same with anyone who will allow Him to. Your past does not dictate your future.

You have greatness locked away inside you. Jesus sees past all the dirt and only sees the treasure that He buried, deep inside of you. God knows what He placed inside each and every one of us. He also knows what the enemy of our souls has done to us to keep us from finding out who we are supposed to be.

The beauty of it is that God specializes in restoring broken vessels and making them vessels of honor. He can take a person who seems hopeless and turn that person's life around in such a way that they no longer look like the same person the next time someone sees them.

Chapter 5

You are a Diamond in the Rough

A diamond doesn't always look like a diamond. It takes years of extreme pressure and intense heat to make a diamond out of a lump of coal. However, that lump of coal always held the potential to become a diamond. The coal, dirty as it may be have always been, was a diamond in the rough. It just had to go through a process and get shined up to become what it was created to be. That's what God does with us if we will allow Him to complete the process. He did that in my life and He will do it for anyone who will trust Him.

No one is so down that the Lord can't pick them back up again. There's not a person on the face of this earth who is so hard-hearted that the love of God can't melt that heart of stone. It's a proven fact that no one is too far gone that the Spirit of God cannot lead them to where they are supposed to be.

At His Feet

King David said it best:

Where can I go from Your Spirit? Or where can I flee from Your presence? 8 If I ascend into heaven, You are there; If I make my bed in hell, behold, You are there. 9 If I take the wings of the morning, And dwell in the uttermost parts of the sea,10Even there Your hand shall lead me, And Your right hand shall hold me.

11 If I say, "Surely the darkness shall fall on me," Even the night shall be light about me; 12 Indeed, the darkness shall not hide from You, But the night shines as the day; The darkness and the light are both alike to You. Psalm 139:7-12 (NKJV)

You may have a friend or family member whose situation looks hopeless. You may have given up any hope that they will ever change. All you are able to see at the moment is the problem, though God sees the solution. Don't give up just yet — because a moment at the feet of Jesus will set in motion a chain of events that will change that person's life forever.

Don't let go of your own faith because faith brings great rewards.

Faith sees past the circumstances and does not look at what is temporary.

Faith looks to the future and sees with spiritual eyes what is yet to come. Your loved one may run from God but they cannot hide. Remember, as for you and your house, you will serve the Lord.

When I found myself at the feet of Jesus the first time, I did not look like the author of a book, a business owner or the pastor of a growing ministry. That didn't matter, however, because that's

At His Feet

exactly who God saw in me. It took me getting past all the wrong mindsets and losing myself to really find out who I was created to be. I had to start seeing myself as God saw me. I was a new creation, the old Angie was dead and gone. It was up to me to stop digging in the graveyard of my past. I was not who the world said I was so I had to shut myself off to all the negative voices speaking death over me. I had to start believing that I was in fact who God said I was. I found my identity in Christ and have changed and grown every day into the person He created me to be. Have I arrived? No, but I press in each day to the High calling of God, found only in who I am in Christ. It's a new day and I am a new person! I grow daily in my relationship with the new lover of my soul and it is a wonderful adventure.

As I continue my story, you learn what happened the second time I found myself **At His Feet**.

At His Feet

Chapter 6

He's in the House

Luke 10:38-42 (NKJV)

38Now it happened as they went that He entered a certain village; and a certain woman named Martha welcomed Him into her house. 39And she had a sister called Mary, who also sat at Jesus' feet and heard His word. 40But Martha was distracted with much serving, and she approached Him and said, "Lord, do You not care that my sister has left me to serve alone? Therefore tell her to help me." 41And Jesus answered and said to her, "Martha, Martha, you are worried and troubled about many things. 42But one thing is needed, and Mary has chosen that good part, which will not be taken away from her."

The second time Mary found herself at the feet of Jesus, He had come to her home. She couldn't believe it! Jesus came to her house for dinner, out of all the places in the city He could have chosen! Mary was beside herself with excitement. She wanted to spend time with Jesus but her sister had other plans for her. Jesus had come to visit Mary but she was stuck in the kitchen with Martha, her over-achieving sister. Martha was a 'Little Miss Fix-It', she's the one who gets things done. The Martha's of the world have a place for everything and everything has to be in its place. The day of Jesus' visit would be no different, everything had to be perfect as Jesus the miracle-working teacher was at Martha's dinner table.

Picture Mary in the kitchen, drying the dishes and complaining

At His Feet

to herself muttering things like, "Why should I be stuck in this kitchen with her? She doesn't know him like I do, she doesn't love him like I do. He never had to rescue her from an angry lynch mob of religious zealots. I have to get out there where he is, I just don't belong in this stupid kitchen!" I imagine her throwing down the dish towel and running into the living room, falling at His feet.

Mary soaked in His every word, completely enthralled with Him. Like a small child opening a Christmas present, the glow on her face could light the entire room. The King of Glory was in her house and she knew He came just to spend time with her.

He was definitely not like any other man she had ever known. Even the way He looked at her was like a father looking at his daughter. This had to be the Son of God because no ordinary man has eyes like His, the average Joe doesn't speak the kind of words He speaks. No Pharisee or rabbi she had known before could teach with the perfect combination of authority and liberty with which He taught.

Yes, Mary had found her first love and nothing was going to make her move from the place she was, at His feet.

Martha, however, was in a panic. How dare her silly sister leave her in the kitchen to do all this work by herself?! After all, didn't she realize Jesus was there? They just had to make a good impression or He wouldn't come back. Besides, she thought, if He were truly a man of God He would know that women were supposed to be cooking and cleaning. It's just not proper for her to be in there at the

At His Feet

feet of the teacher, she thought, and look at her — she looks like a pitiful puppy begging for scraps. Martha decided to put a stop to it before Mary made a fool out of them all.

Martha stormed into the living room. "Jesus, tell her to leave you alone and get in this kitchen and help me. She doesn't know what she's doing. All this silly woman talks about is Jesus, Jesus, Jesus. Tell her she's bothering you and to get in here and do her work. If she doesn't help me then it will take forever to finish and we just won't be on schedule." Martha was so worried about having everything perfect that she didn't realize that the God of all creation was in her living room.

I imagine the Lord saying, "Martha, Martha, you are worrying yourself sick. Take a load off yourself and sit with us a while. Rest, let's talk and get to know one another. Your sister is here learning and that's exactly what she should be doing. I won't take that away from her and make her leave me. However, you can join us if you like."

Infuriated, Martha turns and walks into the kitchen. She was so caught up in doing the work that she was neglecting who she was working for. . .

The second time I found myself at the feet of Jesus was in the same jail but, this time it was different. I had fallen in love with Him and His word. I would spend as much as 16 hours a day reading the Bible and praying to the Lord. The Word had taken on a whole new meaning to me, they were not just empty words from an outdated book. They were alive and just jumping off the pages into the core

At His Feet

of my very being. To me, time in His word was time spent with Him. I soaked up every single page and as I did I was transformed from the person I used to be to the person I became. I found hope and peace hidden in the pages of the Bible. I learned that I was not the first, nor would I be the last, who had obstacles to overcome. However, I now know I was not doing it alone. My faith grew by leaps and bounds and my thoughts were renewed. I didn't even think like the girl who had first come to that jail. I had a positive perspective and I spoke with compassion to those around me. Time spent at the feet of my Savior had totally transformed me.

I remember one special morning I was in my small cell just loving on Jesus. I sang and prayed to my Lord. I may have been in prison but prison was not in me. You can't chain the Word of God or the power of the Holy Ghost!

As I worshiped Him and prayed in the Spirit, I could feel the warm sun shine on me from a 5- by 30-inch window. On the floor in the cold cell, a bunk on one side and a metal toilet on the other, I was full of joy because in the presence of the Almighty God.

In my mind, I saw Jesus standing before me. I saw His feet and the hem of His robe. I reached out and touched Him, crying tears of joy and telling Him how much I loved Him. I touched His feet and touched the hem of His garment. It was so wonderful that I didn't even care that I was going to spend two more years in prison. I was freer than I had ever been; I was with Jesus.

Later that evening I went to the chapel service. One of my

At His Feet

favorite preachers was there, Charlie Abraham, a true prophet of God. I'm telling you God takes this man into your prayer closet and allows him to reveal things to you that only you and God know about.

Well, that morning God took Charlie into my jail cell. In the middle of his preaching he pointed at me and said, "Today when you touched me." I was blown away! I didn't hear anything else Charlie said after that all I could do was cry and think, 'That was you, that was really you Jesus! You were really in that cell with me!' He was manifesting himself to me and I could not believe it! The Lord of Lord and the King of Kings was in my cell and I wanted to stay at His feet forever.

Time and time again Jesus proved Himself to me. I would receive one word after another about my future. One day I went to the chapel and a woman who was full of the power of God, named Tammy Sheppard, called me up to the front. She said, "I speak healing to your body in Jesus' name." The healing virtue came from her and at that very second I was healed of hepatitis C, an incurable disease. This woman became my Mother in Faith and took me under her wing. She spoke into my life while I was incarcerated and would not

At His Feet

let me give up. God used her to train me and equip me with the Word of Faith. She taught me how to break down the Word and apply it to my life.

I was becoming a doer of the Word and not a hearer only. I was learning how to speak life, and how to stand on the Word calling things that are not as though they were, and my faith was growing! Not only that, I started to move in the gifts of the Spirit. Tammy helped me see that the Word I was soaking in, by spending time at His feet, was a powerful weapon when I spoke it out of my mouth. I could speak things into existence with His Word. The power of death and life was in my tongue and I was learning that I was more than a conqueror.

Tammy came in one morning with another precious lady named Missy Webb. Missy was a power house! She was 5 foot nothing with the most beautiful smile I had ever seen. The first time I met her was a year earlier in the same jail when I was there for a short stay. It was in December and it was snowing horribly outside. The jail was on top of a huge mountain and the roads were treacherous. Missy said she started to turn around when the Holy Ghost spoke to her that there was a girl there who needed Missy. Missy obediently drove up that steep mountain answering God's call.

There at the top of that mountain, I sat broken and ashamed in the chapel. Remember, I said that I had been in and out of church all my life. I had even told my pastor I felt the call of God on my life. I'll never forget when she walked in, drops of water on her coat

At His Feet

where the snow had melted. I thought to myself she looked like an angel with that blonde hair and beautiful smile. But what could this tiny little girl tell me that I don't already know?

I knew myself to be a dope-head loser who really messed up my life and that I better turn to Jesus or I would burn in Hell forever. I knew all that, I felt condemnation all my life, I knew I was a no good piece of trash that was Hell-bound. I had already been to every church in my county trying to get help, and all of them together couldn't even cast all the demons I had in me out. Legion had nothing on me — or so I thought.

Missy, however, never said anything of the sort.

When she opened her mouth to pray the Spirit of the Lord swept through that place and blanketed me with peace. She preached a sermon of hope and restoration. She spoke of having a great future and that God was not mad at us. She said He was merciful and loving. I had been taught all my life that God was a vengeful God, who was ready to strike you down. That if you messed up, you were a hypocrite playing church and you might as well quit.

This little lady walked straight up to me and said, "God sent me here just for you today, that's how much He loves you. You are the apple of His eye." She went on to tell me that I knew Him and I had a calling on my life. She said He had a future and a hope waiting on me.

I prayed with her and left with the fire in my Spirit that had burned long ago rekindled. I just didn't know how to fight the good fight. . . **yet!**

At His Feet

Now, on the morning Tammy and Missy came into the chapel together, I was sitting in the front row soaking up the Word like a sponge. I saw something in the ministers that came to the jail and I wanted it, too. I was hungry for the Word and they were feeding my Spirit man.

God knows how to take what was meant to destroy us and turn it for our good — and that's what He was doing in my life. He sent some of the most anointed men and women into my life when I was in the jail. So now I was being taught love and grace, how to be spirit-led and walk in victory.

Missy preached that day on Ezekiel and the valley of dry bones. She told me to speak the Word of God over myself and speak life. After she finished preaching, Tammy started praying. She spoke up and said someone needed to obey God. I knew instantly it was me because I could feel the anointing rising up inside of me. I gave a message in tongues and Missy interpreted it. That was the first time I had stepped out in the gifts of the Spirit and it excited me.

The Bible tells us in **1 Corinthians 12: 31 (NIV) 31Now eagerly desire the greater gifts.** I was eager and had a great desire for even greater gifts. That morning just increased a hunger inside of me that would not go away! I had to know Jesus more, I had to stay at His feet and learn from Him as much as I could be taught.

Satan had different plans for me. He thought if he could stir up trouble for me I would give up and quit.

At His Feet

Mark 4:17(NIV) But since they have no root, they last only a short time. When trouble or persecution comes because of the word, they quickly fall away.

What I didn't know was that stepping out in faith not only draws God's attention but also draws the enemy's attention as well. The enemy comes immediately to steal the Word. I went back to the cell with the same women who I was incarcerated with for months. They started mocking me, trying to pick fights and even made death threats on my life. Satan was angry and using them as his pawns to get to me. I went from living in peace to living in hell. It had gotten so bad I contemplated being moved to a protective custody unit.

The devil was attacking me in order to stop me from ever coming to the place God had called me to be. He didn't get his way, I drew closer to God in prayer and worship. Sometimes as I would pray I would feel a breeze across my face. I called my mother and she told me that a local minister had been praying for me. The woman told my mother to tell me that if I could only see with my spiritual eyes there were angels encamped around me. Everywhere I went angels were there with their swords drawn. That there had even been times I could feel the wind from their wings on my face. After that day the persecution didn't have a stronghold on me because I knew I was protected.

Chapter 7

Flesh vs. Spirit

Do you remember how it was after you were first saved and could not get enough of Jesus? You would spend countless hours praying and reading His Word. Everywhere you went you had to tell somebody about this wonderful gift of salvation and the man who made it possible. You were on fire and ready to take on the world and every devil in Hell in His name. You had a smile on your face and a song on your lips. You had found your first love in a new relationship with Jesus Christ! Life had taken on a new meaning. You were hungry for the things of God.

Many are still there, however, for many that passion slowly dwindles away. Then little by little the hunger starts to drift away as well and the excitement they once had is gone. Perhaps they decide that they have simply outgrown being so silly.

The sad truth is that for many they have just lost their first love. The fire is almost out and they are caught up in the works of religiosity. They still go to church, they do everything that is expected of them and more. They just don't feel the way they used to feel. They settle for less than God's best and find themselves living mediocre lives. They become satisfied at being the church of status quo and don't want anyone changing their routine.

These people really get mad when some gung-ho new convert comes in and all you hear from that convert is, "We need to do

At His Feet

something more in this church to get the message out to the lost."

Or, "We need to bring in some new, modern music and get this place jumping!"

As our relationship with the Lord gets questioned by these newcomers and they are making ripples in our calm stagnant services, we want to choke them because they really get under our skin. So in our religious "godly" way we talk some sense into them and tell them why that just will not work. When all we are really saying is, I like the way things are and if it ain't broke don't fix it. We have grown cold and are stuck in a religious routine.

Maybe you are a new Christian and have fallen in love with Jesus for the first time. I want to encourage you to stay in the Word and soak it in. Let Him transform you as you sit at His feet. There are things you will learn sitting at his feet, in that intimate alone time with Him, that only He can teach you. You were created for a relationship with the Lord. He loves you with an everlasting love and the more time you spend with Him the stronger your love for Him will grow.

Just as your love for Jesus and His Word grows stronger, you too will grow stronger. When persecution arises — and it will arise — you will not be moved. You will learn how to walk in the spirit and not be overcome by the flesh.

Some may call you radical or strange but that's okay! We are a peculiar people. People who are not walking in a close relationship with the Lord cannot and will not understand you. You have moved from darkness to light, and your light exposes their darkness. You have been transformed from carnal to spiritual and those without the spirit can't understand you. They are living after the dictatorship of their flesh, some are even Christians, carnal but still in the body of believers.

Martha represents the flesh and Mary represents the Spirit.

Martha is steeped in works and Mary is full of the Spirit.

> **Galatians 4:29 (NKJV) But as then he that was born after the flesh persecuted him that was born after the Spirit, even so it is now.**

Martha was angry and persecuting Mary because Martha had gotten so caught up in works she, Martha, had forgotten what is was to walk in the spirit.

Martha had lost the freedom to just flow in the complete adoration of who Jesus was. She had gotten herself entangled in works of Christianity. She was agitated and aggravated when she would see Mary just 'sitting' there doing nothing. In return, Martha persecuted Mary and tried to put a stop to Mary's foolishness.

How many times have we seen this happen in the churches of today? If the church down the road does something different or someone tries to change the way we do things in our own church, we become angry and frustrated. In return, we start trying to shut them down and use the Word to do it.

The end-times church is not a modern church nor is it a traditional church. It is a group of believers, functioning together as His body. We need to be a mixture of Mary and Martha! Then we will see a move of God in our church. Many get so caught up in doing they forget who they are doing it for. Then on the other hand we see people who sit and do nothing.

The radical Christian is one on fire for God, worshipping as they are working! We need the body of Christ coming together and worshipping together in spirit and truth.

There is also the social gospel club type of church. It's the ones who have great music and huge attendance. But, they preach an itching ear message and never get the members off the bottle. So we have a bunch of carnal Christians walking around cheapening the grace of God.

Grace is not a license to sin as many have made it out to be. Grace is unmerited favor, but, it's is also the power of God made available to His bride to live holy lives. God is looking for worshipers to worship in spirit and the truth of His Word. Doing what He says to do, crucifying the flesh and walking in the spirit. They are not moved by the persecution that comes their way, they know that God is for them and no one can successfully be against them.

There are churches rising up all over the world that are not satisfied with everyday church as we know it. They are not seeker friendly, nor are they overbearing and pharisaical. The last days church is a multi-generational, multi-cultural church. They are not bound by religious traditions nor do they use grace as a license to sin. They are a body of believers coming together in unity with one thing on their mind: Jesus, and seeing His Kingdom come in all

At His Feet

its majesty!

This church is not settling for status quo, they are standing on His word and seeking His face! This church knows their Lord, they are strong in Him and are doing exploits in His name.

The time of miracles has not passed away! God has a remnant of believers who are walking in the miraculous with signs and wonders following. They are walking in the spirit and denying their fleshly appetites — not living a compromised life.

This apostolic church is equipping the saints and placing those saints into their God-given callings! They are the ones who will usher in the return of the Lord!

At His Feet

Chapter 8

Delays are not Denials

John 11:32-44 New King James Version (NKJV)

32 Then, when Mary came where Jesus was, and saw Him, she fell down at His feet, saying to Him, "Lord, if You had been here, my brother would not have died."

33 Therefore, when Jesus saw her weeping, and the Jews who came with her weeping, He groaned in the spirit and was troubled. 34And He said, "Where have you laid him?"

They said to Him, "Lord, come and see."

35 Jesus wept. 36 Then the Jews said, "See how He loved him!" 37And some of them said, "Could not this Man, who opened the eyes of the blind, also have kept this man from dying?"

38 Then Jesus, again groaning in Himself, came to the tomb. It was a cave, and a stone lay against it. 39 Jesus said,

"Take away the stone."

The third time Mary found herself at the feet of Jesus, her dear

brother, Lazarus, had died. She expected her Lord to come

and heal Lazarus. After all, she sent for Jesus and Jesus had never

let her down before. Jesus had always been there in the past, every

time she ever needed Him, Jesus was there.

Every time except this time.

Imagine her running to Jesus and falling at His feet once again,

crying out, "Lord if only you had shown up my brother would not

At His Feet

have died! Why didn't you come when we called for you? You could have saved him and now he's dead!"

Mary was understandably hurt and confused. She trusted Jesus and couldn't understand why He didn't come when she sent for Him. The messenger came back with the word that Jesus had been told about her brother's illness. Jesus had plenty of time to make it there before Lazarus died. Why didn't he come? Didn't he care anymore? What could have been the reason he would avoid their plea for help? Regardless, by then it was too late. Lazarus was dead and gone and Mary would never see her dear brother again.

However she was still at the feet of Jesus. She ran out to worship Him like she had so many times before. Crying out to Him in her pain something inside of her knew He still had all the answers and somehow He could ease her pain.

I had been moved from the South Western Regional Jail to the Lakin Correctional Facility, a prison in West Columbia, West Virginia. All that time I was standing on the Word of God, growing strong in Spirit.

Several of the ministers God placed in my life at SWRJ were ministers at Lakin Correctional Facility as well. God was blessing me even behind prison walls. Every need was being met and I was even given the opportunity to work outside of my cell. I was in prison but I had a new freedom that I hadn't had in the 10 months at the jail.

I was in the recreation yard one morning when a call came over the intercom for me. I was instructed to return to my cell, put on my

At His Feet

sweat suit and come to booking.

I saw two Tazewell County police officers with hand cuffs, there to take me to face charges in Virginia. I had only been at Lakin for 18 months but it was time for me to be sentenced for charges I committed in Virginia, as well. I knew even though I was extradited to Virginia, I would have to come back to Lakin for my parole hearing. However, I had the Faith of Abraham. I knew I had been standing on God's word for two years and He could not lie. He was going to set me free and I knew it! I trusted Him and His word said that those who trusted Him will never be put to shame.

Jesus breaks into pieces the bars of iron and sets captives free, so I knew in my heart that I would not get any more time in Virginia and that I would make parole in West Virginia.

I felt that two years was a long enough penalty for writing fraudulent checks. After all, I had repented and changed my ways. Why wouldn't He set me free! I knew God was going to perform a miracle for me like He did for Paul and Silas when they were thrown in jail. I was coming out of there into my new future!

I found myself in Tazewell County Jail where I spent three months awaiting trial. I worked in laundry so that gave me time to be alone and read my Bible. The guys in the kitchen cooked good food for the laundry workers; food the other inmates didn't get to eat. So once again I found favor.

I'll never forget the morning I was sentenced.

It was Good Friday. I was in the holding cell praying in the spirit. The guards and other inmates could hear me all over that place. I prayed and said, "Jesus you are my substitute, on this day over 2000 years ago you were standing before Pontius Pilot and the Sanhedrin for me. You took my place and were crucified on this day so I could be set free. You hold the heart of that judge in your hands. I'm asking you to set me free."

2 Corinthians 4:8-9

New King James Version (NKJV)

8 We are hard-pressed on every side, yet not crushed; we are perplexed, but not in despair; 9 persecuted, but not forsaken; struck down, but not destroyed—

I stood alone in front of the judge with a lawyer who ironically never really seemed to be on my side. Even though I had evidence that I did not steal the checks I had written, he never spoke a word in my defense. I was sentenced to two more years consecutive with the two I was pulling in West Virginia.

I was crushed, but not enough to give up. I still trusted Jesus even though I was confused. I knew there must be a reason that He didn't let me go.

I went back to the cell and picked up my Bible and started reading. The other inmates couldn't believe I wasn't cursing. Most of the other women they had seen in prison gave up on Jesus after receiving their sentence. All they had ever seen was what they called "jail house religion".

Two days later, on Easter Sunday, I was given the chance to

At His Feet

preach my first full sermon. I preached to about 30 women in a jail chapel. I knew God had a plan and there was a reason I was sentenced to two more years. I also knew I could handle whatever they threw my way. I was more than a conqueror and delays are not denials.

I was then transferred to another jail in Virginia. It was by far the worst facility I had ever experienced. The jailers were cruel and would do anything they could to add to your punishment. You were a number to them and they enjoyed playing games with your emotions. They only gave you clean clothes twice a week. To get the clean clothing you had to stand in line wearing only your underwear to receive the bundled clothes through a small pie hole in the door. If one inmate angered the jailors, the jailers would lock every inmate out of her cell in the day room for the rest of the day.

We would stay in the day room until that particular shift was over, sitting on the floor because there were not enough seats for everyone. We went without toilet paper or even a cup to drink water from. I believe dogs get better treatment.

However, out of all the bad, God always had a blessing for me. I went to a chapel service one night and saw two familiar faces from my childhood. It was my step-father's sister-in-law Dana, and her sister Colleen. Dana was teaching the Word and Colleen was singing with the voice of an angel. Colleen is an on-air personality on WIVK Radio in Knoxville, Tennessee. I was instantly drawn to them.

At His Feet

I recalled Colleen singing to me and Dana's daughter when we were just children. I was beyond happy to see them in that dark place. They encouraged me during those services and told me they knew God had something special in store for me. It's funny how the Father orders our steps and makes something so ugly turn into something oh-so-beautiful.

I was only in that horrific place for a month before I was sent back to Lakin to serve out the rest of my West Virginia sentence. I was back with the ministers I loved so much. Tammy, of course, and Billy and Sabrina Manuel. They encouraged me every week. Those ministers taught me to walk in faith and stand on God's Word. They showed me love and friendship like I had never known before. This was not just inmate/minister relationships, God was forming bonds that would last throughout the rest of my life.

Deuteronomy 1:6-8

2King James Version (KJV)

6 The Lord our God spoke unto us in Horeb, saying,

Ye have dwelt long enough in this mountain.

When the time came for my parole hearing, I was in my new room at Lakin. This was not a cell, it was like a dorm room. I had been accepted into the Four Paws dog training program. That provided me with a dog named Chico as a roommate, and I also had a human roommate from my hometown. Our room even had its own bathroom with a bathtub and real doors with handles.

At His Feet

You should have seen me standing in front of that door the first morning I was in that room. The chow (meal) call had been given and I stood and waited for the guards to buzz me out. My roommate laughed and told me to twist the handle. I hadn't touched a door handle in two years, I wasn't used to it.

This was the executive suite of prison. I sat there watching TV waiting for them to call me to the board room when a minister, Paula White, came onscreen and said, "You have been on that mountain long enough." I felt that was a sign I was going to make parole.

I went into the hearing full of hope and saw my Dad waiting for me. He, my step-mother and little brother all came to support me. After hearing all that I had accomplished the parole board granted me parole on my 2- to 20-year sentence. I cried like a baby, knowing God was for me. I walked down the hall that day singing the song, 'He's an on time God'.

Later that week I went to my last chapel service at Lakin. Billy Manuel was preaching that night. When I told him I was leaving after two years he started to cry. He told me we would see each other again on the outside under better conditions. He and his precious wife Sabrina had been true friends and I hoped I would see them again. Billy reassured me that I was going to be just fine and to hold on to my faith in Jesus with everything I had. The Lord had shown Billy I was about to go through a time of great testing.

At His Feet

Isaiah 42:9

King James Version (KJV)

9Behold, the former things are come to pass, and new things do I declare: before they spring forth I tell you of them.

Later that week I was walking the dog on the recreation yard and the Holy Spirit spoke to me and told me Virginia Corrections was there to get me. In His still small voice He said, "Do not be afraid, I am with you."

The guards called for me and told me to pack all my things. I did as I was told and said my goodbyes to all the girls I had grown to love. It was hard leaving them but it was even harder leaving my Chaplain, Mark.

Chaplain Mark was a wonderful man. He was more of a Pastor than all the prison evangelist I had known. He always taught us the importance of Family and unity in the Body. He loved us like a Father loves his daughters, and we loved him.

As I was at the door leaving I insisted they call for Chaplain Mark. He came in a hurry to see me off. I vividly remember the love in his eyes when I told him I didn't want to leave Lakin. He shook my hand and said, "I don't want you to leave either." This man showed me what a true Pastor is supposed to be like.

He was much different from my Chaplain at the jail. Mark Miller, the chaplain at SWRJ, was someone who could make me laugh when I wanted to cry. He preached at Lakin a lot, too. He

At His Feet

always talked about the joy of the Lord. He taught me that I could have fun serving Jesus and didn't have to walk on egg shells all the time. He taught me the love and mercy of a forgiving Father, and how I should show mercy to those around me. He would say, "There's too many good things in the Bible and you for me to point out all the bad. When you feel good about yourself, you do good with yourself." I use that with my congregation to this day. Pastors love and protect their sheep. The shepherd's rod and staff was to protect the sheep and beat the wolves away; not the other way around.

Until Lakin I thought Pastors were supposed to be harsh and distant, Bible-beating you over everything you did wrong. Every lesson Chaplain Mark taught me about being a pastor I now use at my church.

At His Feet

Chapter 9

God, Where are You?

The time had come to leave Lakin behind forever. Three days after that I found myself thrown once again at the feet of Jesus. I was taken to Fluvanna Correctional Center where I was once again stripped of all my dignity and self-worth. This had to be the closest place to hell on the face of the earth.

When I arrived, I had black curly hair that reached below my waist, one of the few things about myself I had always considered beautiful. The facilitators insisted it be cut completely off. In Virginia, women have to cut their hair and are treated more like animals than humans.

Not only did I have two years left to serve in that place but I was informed that none of the three months I spent in Tazewell would be counted towards my sentence. Additionally, nine more months were tacked onto my existing two-year sentence. How could I make it? What had gone wrong?

I retreated to a cell frightened and alone, crying out to Jesus, "Why Lord, why? If you wanted to you could have sent me home. If only you had showed up. Did you not hear me? You said your word would not return void! You said you set captives free. I have done everything I am supposed to do. I was alright with two more years. But I can't handle this. You've got to do something!"

I felt like Mary at the tomb. I knew Jesus had the power to bring life but he was late. He hadn't shown up for me this time and I could not understand why.

God knows the end from the beginning. He knew exactly what He was doing in my life. Our Father was more concerned with breaking some spiritual chains off of me than with my release from a temporary situation. He was trying my faith, as I believe he did with Mary.

Do you remember, He said,

"Am I not the resurrection and the life?"

He was setting an emotional captive free and training a spiritual warrior.

At His Feet

Isaiah 48:10-11

New King James Version (NKJV)

10 Behold, I have refined you, but not as silver;

I have tested you in the furnace of affliction.

11 For My own sake, for My own sake, I will do it;

For how should My name be profaned?

And I will not give My glory to another.

We are refined in the fire and I found myself in the hottest part of the furnace. I was guaranteed to come out of that place a different person. God made sure I could see what was really in my heart. When we go through the Refiner's fire, all the impurities come to the surface. I still had a lot of junk inside my heart and God needed to make sure I saw it. He had to purge me of insecurities, fears, pride and anything else that would keep me from becoming a vessel of honor.

I was still bound by some things from my past. God wanted to change my way of thinking and completely renew my mind. I was a new creation but I was still holding on to the tomb. He had to keep me in the fire until the chains that had tied me to my past were completely melted away.

Just as He did for Moses and the Israelites, my Father was taking me into the Promised Land so he had to make sure that I was thinking like a daughter instead of a slave. Egypt mentality has no place in the Promised Land. God wanted to make sure I had what it took to make it on the outside, beyond the prison walls. He wanted to be able to

At His Feet

use me in the future to help others with the same issues I had dealt with. I had to learn to think like a new creation instead of the like the old Angela. Jesus is never late, he always comes right on time. Some wonder, why does God allow things to come upon his children and He seems to be far away when it does? In many cases He does this so we will see what He sees inside our hearts. When our Father does the exact opposite of what we have asked Him to do our true character shows up. Many times it is not very nice.

When God doesn't answer on our time clock or do what we think he should do we start murmuring, complaining or just downright sinning. Many people fall away during times of testing. I want to encourage you today if you are in a season of testing: please don't fall away, fall at His feet. He is creating a vessel of honor and He will not give His glory to another.

Chapter 10

The Tomb of Your Past

Romans 4:17 (ASV)

17 (as it is written, A father of many nations have I made thee) before him whom he believed, even God, who giveth life to the dead, and calleth the things that are not, as though they were.

Some hear Jesus calling them right now to step out of the tombs of their past. These people were once alive but something took place over the years to destroy their dreams and kill their visions. He is bringing life back to those people. I can hear him yelling in the spiritual realm, "Lazarus come forth! It's time for you to live again!" Let him use the fire of his Holy Spirit to remove your grave clothes and let you go free!

He isn't finished with you yet. He is restoring the visions you once had and giving you a new zeal. Times of refreshing are coming if you will leave the tomb and step out into the brand new day. God knows what He's doing in your life. He knows where He is taking you and knows exactly how to get you there. Trust Him to get you through the process. God is using these times and seasons to teach us to trust Him and not lean on our own understanding. Those who trust Him will never be put to shame and those who seek Him will never lack anything good.

Are we going to be like Mary and fall at His feet when we are hurt and confused? Or are we going to run away in anger and fall prey to the enemy?

At His Feet

Jesus is telling us today the same thing He told Mary: If you will only believe, your brother will live again.

He wants you to know if you only believe in Him, your dreams will live again. This sickness will not end in death. This marriage will not end in divorce. This company will not go bankrupt. This child will not die lost.

Jesus is saying to you now, "Whatever it is you are believing me for, hold on! I am the resurrection and the life! This is not the end it's just the beginning! Trust me and fall at my feet! Life and health is coming. Prosperity and deliverance are on the way. Believe me and blessings will come upon and over take you!"

God used the hardest time of my life to make the greatest change inside of me. You see, the Refiner never takes His eyes off of what He is refining. The Potter never takes his eyes off the clay. He knows exactly how much heat to apply and when to take the clay out and let it cool.

I was moved from Fluvanna, the maximum security facility, within three months and taken to Goochland, an open facility. There I was given several different jobs. I was taught to do a variety of things, from running a weed eater to driving heavy equipment. I even earned my certification in horticulture and now own a landscaping business thanks to it.

Delays are not denials. He is an on time God and knows exactly what He's doing. Not only had I learned a natural trade that would benefit me in life, I learned patience. God was teaching me the lost

At His Feet

art of waiting on Him. I also learned how to fight the good fight of faith. The Father was turning me into a vessel He could use for His glory.

At His Feet

Chapter 11

The Heart of Worship

Luke 7:36-47

New King James Version (NKJV)

36 Then one of the Pharisees asked Him to eat with him. And He went to the Pharisee's house, and sat down to eat. 37And behold, a woman in the city who was a sinner, when she knew that Jesus sat at the table in the Pharisee's house, brought an alabaster flask of fragrant oil, 38 and stood at His feet behind Him weeping; and she began to wash His feet with her tears, and wiped them with the hair of her head; and she kissed His feet and anointed them with the fragrant oil. 39Now when the Pharisee who had invited Him saw this, he spoke to himself, saying, "This Man, if He were a prophet, would know who and what manner of woman this is who is touching Him, for she is a sinner."

40And Jesus answered and said to him, "Simon,

I have something to say to you."

So he said, "Teacher, say it."

41 "There was a certain creditor who had two debtors. One owed five hundred denarii, and the other fifty. 42And when they had nothing with which to repay, he freely forgave them both. Tell Me, therefore, which of them will love him more?"

43 Simon answered and said, "I suppose the

one whom he forgave more."

And He said to him, "You have rightly judged." 44 Then He turned

At His Feet

> to the woman and said to Simon, "Do you see this woman? I entered your house; you gave Me no water for My feet, but she has washed My feet with her tears and wiped them with the hair of her head. 45 You gave Me no kiss, but this woman has not ceased to kiss My feet since the time I came in. 46 You did not anoint My head with oil, but this woman has anointed My feet with fragrant oil. 47 Therefore I say to you, her sins, which are many, are forgiven, for she loved much. But to whom little is forgiven,
>
> the same loves little."

The final time we read of Mary at the feet of Jesus was when she anointed him for his burial. In those days, the only people who were anointed were the Kings, the Priests and the dead. Jesus was her King, He was her teacher and High Priest and she knew deep down in her heart He was not going to be with her for much longer. Something on the inside of her screamed that they were about to kill her Lord.

She had to be with Him one last time. She had to show Him how much she loved Him. So she gathered up her most prized possession and went to find Jesus.

She searched high and low until she got word of His whereabouts. He was at the home of one of the Pharisees. She knew she didn't belong there, as women were not welcomed in those types of places. Mary was especially unwelcome; everyone there would remember who she was and where she came from. These were the same men who so viciously dragged her to his feet the first time.

At His Feet

However, she would not allow anything to stop her from getting to Jesus. She pushed her way through a room full of men, ignoring their remarks towards her. She didn't care what they said nor did she care what they might do to her. She was not going to let anything stop her from getting to Jesus.

Mary fell at the feet of this precious man and began weeping uncontrollably. She poured her worship onto the man who had changed her life. Her tears fell on His feet and washed away all the dirt the day's journey had left there. She took her long black hair and dried Jesus' feet, wiping away any trace of dirt that was left behind. She loved Jesus more than life itself. How could she go on without Him? She reached into her bag and pulled out an alabaster jar of perfumed oil. She began to anoint his head and feet. I can imagine the oil flowing over his long black hair and beard.

The perfumed oils of that time cost a fortune. Mary's life savings went to purchase that alabaster jar. Everything she had sold her body for, everything she could save, all that she had as far as material wealth; she used it to purchase that oil. The cost was an entire year's wages for some people. Yet she poured it out onto the one who meant more to her than anything money could buy.

The religious men never even gave Jesus water to wash his feet as was custom in that time period. Imagine Mary massaging the oil into the Savior's dry and cracked feet. Bathing His feet in her precious, valuable, perfumed oil; Mary continued to worship and tell Him how much she loved Him.

At His Feet

John 4:24

New King James Version (NKJV)

24 God is Spirit, and those who worship Him must worship in spirit and truth."

God looks for people today to worship like Mary did then. The worship she brought to Jesus was from a pure heart with pure motives. She wasn't offering lip service, she was giving Him her entire heart. The flask she broke to pour the oil out represents our flesh. For worship to be genuine it has to come from broken flesh and a humble heart. Nothing done in the flesh is true worship.

Many people offer worship with their mouth but their heart is far from Him. Religious worship from half-hearted people coming from half-hearted lips is not pleasing to God. It does not attract His attention. God inhabits the praise of His people, so to have the kind of worship God longs to live in we worship with pure hearts and broken flesh.

Mary loved Jesus. Where there is much forgiveness there is much love. I imagine her crying and telling Jesus over and over again, "I Love you my Lord. Thank you Jesus, thank you for everything you've done for me."

How long has it been since we poured our worship out on Him like oil? Since we came into His presence with nothing on our hearts but loving for Him? Not asking for anything except to be near Him? eyes of the Lord are searching the Body of Christ, looking for people who just want Him. When He finds a heart like that He will

At His Feet

move Heaven and Earth to bless that person. This kind of worship makes our King happy; when we want nothing more than Him, when nothing will satisfy us but Him!

Mary's appearance in the Pharisee's home, the 'religious' men had to have thought, "If Jesus knew what kind of women this was He would never allow this kind of trash to touch him." However, Jesus did know Mary and she knew him. Mary had a relationship with Jesus that these men would never have. Jesus knew her heart and knew it was pure. He also knew how foul those men's hearts had become. There is a huge difference between religion and relationship. Those men could never understand Mary's worship because they could not understand her heart. They did not understand love and devotion to the King. These were the kind of men the Bible speaks about in **Matthew 15:8, "They worship me with their mouth, but, their heart is far from me."**

Can you imagine the wonderful smell in that room after Mary broke open the perfume oil and poured it out on the Master? Her worship was even sweeter. Mary's worship went before the King of Glory like a sweet smelling aroma! Her worship covered all the stench that was in that room; the spiritual stench of pride and greed coming from the men in the room that day.

That's what true worship does today! True worship goes before the Father into the throne room and covers the stench of the world! There is nothing the Father will not do for a true worshipper. He will move Heaven and Earth to bless someone who wants nothing but

At His Feet

Him! When we seek the Blesser, the blessings will chase us down.

Philippians 3:18-20

New International Version (NIV)

18For, as I have often told you before and now tell you again even with tears, many live as enemies of the cross of Christ. 19 Their destiny is destruction, their god is their stomach, and their glory is in their shame. Their mind is set on earthly things. 20But our citizenship is in heaven. And we eagerly await a Savior from there, the Lord Jesus Christ.

Judas, one of Jesus' disciples, was infuriated that Mary wasted the expensive oil. He wanted it sold so the money from the proceeds could go into the treasury. He yelled out, "What is going on here? Look at this waste, this could have been sold and given to the poor." Judas wasn't worried about Jesus. He didn't care about Mary or the poor. He was a thief and had been stealing money from the treasury for a long time by then.

It is sad to say that even today there are people behind church walls who do not care about Jesus or His people. Those individuals believe God is in their bellies and all they care about is self. They are in it for what they can gain from it!

Some want to build a name for themselves, instead of lifting high the name of Jesus. It's a 'look at me' mentality. With every action they seem to ask, "What about me, don't you see me? **Ta da! Here I am!**" This is the same attitude that Judas had. This attitude gave Satan access to Judas' life. This kind of evil is what lead to the betrayal of Jesus!

At His Feet

We must be on guard to keep our hearts from getting full of pride and greed. If ministry is about ourselves and not about Jesus then we are walking on dangerous ground. We should never think more highly of ourselves or of our calling than Who called upon us. We should never look to see what we can gain from being in a ministry position. Our focus must remain on Jesus and the people He has given us! He must increase and we must decrease.

The church needs to get back to the heart of worship. God is looking for worshipers who will worship out of their love for Him. The Father doesn't want our praise due to an inflated ego or desire to gain something from us. He wants us to worship Him with a pure heart so He can make provision for us. Worship opens doors to many blessings we would otherwise never receive.

Mary wanted nothing more than to love her Lord. That's where our heart should be as well. When we draw near to Him in worship everything else dims in comparison. God reveals Himself to us as we worship and the things of this world no longer seem to matter.

The closer we draw to His Holy Flame the more we become like Him. That allows Him to show up and show off in our lives. Like I said before, there is nothing God will not do for a worshipper.

At His Feet

James 1:2-4

New Living Translation (NLT)

Faith and Endurance

2 Dear brothers and sisters,[a] when troubles come your way, consider it an opportunity for great joy. 3For you know that when your faith is tested, your endurance has a chance to grow. 4 So let it grow, for when your endurance is fully developed, you will be perfect and complete, needing nothing.

Finally the big day arrived; the day I would finally get to go home after four long years in prison.

My mother bought me new clothes and mailed them to me. She had sprayed the new coat with her own perfume which smelled wonderful

in that musky old prison. I fixed my hair, put on my make-up and was ready to start my new life as a free woman.

My dad was waiting in the front office as I signed my release papers. I couldn't believe I was finally going home! My dad drove around to get me and my belongings at the front gate. As he pulled up and I was getting ready to step into his GMC Denali, a prison guard grabbed my wrist.

"You can't go anywhere," the guard said, "There's a hold on you from Russell County, Virginia, and the Sheriff's Office is on the way here to pick you up."

I couldn't believe it. I thought it was some kind of sick joke, probably one of the cruelest things that had ever happened to me. How could they allow me to get one step away from freedom then

At His Feet

spring this on me?

I recall so vividly the look on my dad's face and the tears that spilled from his eyes. He was devastated. I, too, was crushed but my faith was not destroyed. I was stronger than I had ever been. I knew in Whom I had believed and that no matter where I was He was with me! I trusted Him!

The officers returned me to the worst jail I had been in, the one I screamed and pleaded with God to deliver me from. This time I praised and worshiped him. I found myself once again at His feet. I remember being in my cell and telling my Lord, "Father, you know this hurts, I don't understand why this happened. But I choose to trust you. No matter what happens, I will serve you."

For three days I witnessed and praised the Lord. I prayed for women at the jail and encouraged them to put their trust in the Lord. I went to my cell at night and worshiped through my tears. I found out the true meaning of offering up a sacrifice of praise. I would worship my Master no matter what.

I was told I had to serve nine more months. However, God had the final say.

On the third morning, I received a call.

"Angela," the voice said, "pack your things, you are going home!" moved on the heart of the judge to send me home. God had proven me faithful, I had passed the final test. I was now ready to live life on the outside.

That was only the beginning of what he had done for me.

At His Feet

Proverbs 16:7

King James Version (KJV)

7 When a man's ways please the Lord, he maketh even his enemies to be at peace with him.

One month later I had to go before the judge for a final hearing. I walked in with my family and the same lawyer who never tried to defend me any of the other times. This time, I knew in my heart everything was going to be in my favor. God was with me.

The Judge asked my attorney to state the reasons I should be released. My attorney's exact words were, "Your Honor, as you can tell, Angela looks like a changed person. But looks can be deceiving, we will just have to see."

I was in shock. My dad looked at him like he wanted to hit him. The truth is, I wanted to hit him, too.

The judge asked me to take the stand and tell him my plans for the future. Boy, did I ever! I told him my plans to go into full time ministry and help others find freedom from drug addiction. I told him that while I was in jail I had given my heart to Jesus and was now a changed woman.

Lawyers often advise against speaking of your faith because they say everyone finds Jesus in prison. They call it 'jail house religion', and are adamant that the judge has heard it all before.

I didn't let that stop me. I told of my faith in Christ and the plans He had for my future. My dad was even looking at me, shaking his

At His Feet

head to warn me to stop blowing it. I couldn't help it; when I opened my mouth before that judge, God filled it.

I got off the stand and the atmosphere in the court room was so thick you could cut it with a knife. The judge asked the prosecutor if she knew any reason that I should go back to jail.

The prosecutor, a woman, stood and said, "Yes your Honor, I have something to say. Mrs. Matney [my last name was Matney at the time] has done everything that the State of Virginia would like for an inmate to do. She has taken advantage of every opportunity given her. She has completed a two year Theraputical Community program, all while working a full time job and going to school. She has been certified in Horticulture and the State of Virginia is very proud of her." The prosecutor then sat down.

2 Chronicles 16:9

King James Version (KJV)

9For the eyes of the Lord run to and fro throughout the whole earth, to show himself strong in the behalf of them whose heart is perfect toward him.

I was blown away!

That is how God does things for His people. The person who should have taken up for me became my Judas and the person who should have been my enemy became my defender. Who but God does that? Nobody!

The judge stood and said, "Mrs. Matney, you are free to go!"

I left that day never to return. Who the Son sets free is Free

At His Feet

indeed! My God had shown Himself strong on my behalf.

I went home that day with a deeper level of faith. I knew that there was nothing impossible to me. If God says it, He will do it.

Chapter 12

Worshiping Your Way to Victory!

Psalm 37:4

New King James Version (NKJV)

4 Delight yourself also in the Lord,

And He shall give you the desires of your heart.

I want to encourage you today to Worship God no matter what the circumstances look like. When all seems lost and it's as if all Hell has broken loose against you, worship your way to victory. Even when you cannot see the light at the end of the tunnel, open your mouth and praise Him; you will see the Glory of the Lord shining through the darkness. Your praise will confuse your enemies and bring victory from defeat. God is no respecter of persons; what He did for me, He will do for you.

You may be facing a different type of enemy. Your enemy may be sickness or poverty. You may have lost your job or have a drug addicted family member. You may be bound by some type of besetting sin.

It doesn't matter what the enemy is, it's no match for Jesus. And it's no match for you! Greater is He that's in you because it's Christ who lives on the inside. Fall at His feet and worship Him with everything you have in you. Open your mouth in praise and the Lion of the Tribe of Judah will begin to roar on the inside of you! Your enemies will fall back in terror and you will soon find you are more

At His Feet

than a conqueror through Christ.

Whatever it is that you need today, you will find it at the feet of Jesus. He loves you and wants to pour blessings out on you. The key to the open door you need, is in seeking the King through His word. Do what it says and worship Him with all of your heart. You will find the life you've always wanted **At His Feet**!

At His Feet

Chapter 13

Beauty for Ashes

Isaiah 61:3

New King James Version (NKJV)

3 To console those who mourn in Zion,

To give them beauty for ashes,

The oil of joy for mourning,

The garment of praise for the spirit of heaviness;

That they may be called trees of righteousness,

The planting of the Lord, that He may be glorified.

After my release from prison I have found myself on numerous occasions at my master's feet. He has always welcomed me and even longs to find me there, as He does you.

I believe at His feet is where we find our purpose for being alive. It is where he transforms us into His image and showers us in His love. At His feet we lose ourselves yet find who we really are. Our true identity can only be found in Christ.

Jesus has truly given me Beauty for Ashes and taken what Satan meant for evil turning it for my good. For everything I lived through until now God has given me double recompense. He has been so merciful and loving. I do not even have words to describe the magnitude

of His blessings on my life.

At His Feet

I am now the wife of a wonderful Man of God who loves me more than I deserve. I am a mother again and have a beautiful baby girl. My other children have been restored to my life. My husband and I pastor a wonderful church of hungry revivalists. Within two years of my release God has given me a home of my own, and a thriving ministry.

We have pioneered many ministries in WV. Including opening the 1st sober living homes in McDowell County.   He has opened the doors to my hearts desires and given me everything I have asked Him for. I have even been allowed to become a part of one of the biggest prison ministries in the United States.

God has provided exceedingly above my wildest dreams and I will forever praise Him. Not because He has done all these wonderful things for me, but because I love Him. Where there is much forgiveness there is much love. He opened my eyes to see who He created me to be. I am not the trash the world wanted me to believe I was. **I am a daughter of the King**!

At His Feet

I believe Joyce Meyer said it best when she said, "God turns a test into a testimony, a mess into a message." That is exactly what He has done in my life.

God did not bless me because I deserved it, but because of His mercy and grace. He did it so I could share my story and help others who are suffering through the same things in their life's journeys.

Chapter 14

Divine Connections

Psalm 37:23

New King James Version (NKJV)

23 The steps of a good man are ordered by the Lord,

And He delights in his way.

I have heard that God brings people into our lives for either a reason, a season or a lifetime. I whole-heartedly believe that. The people in my journey were lessons on what to do and what not to do. Many have come and gone, though some will remain until we go to be with Jesus.

Do you remember I told you about God forming life-long friendships between the jail ministers and myself? I have been in contact with almost every one of them and many of them are my best friends today. God orders our steps and places us with the right people at the right time. I like to call them 'divine connections'. There are many more wonderful people God has placed into my life through my relationship with these awesome men and women of God.

Sure, there were plenty of people who had hurt me, betrayed me or abused me — but God replaced them all with people who love me unconditionally. He gave me friends I can trust with my life. Satan can never outdo God. For every wrong person the devil placed in my path, God sent two of the right ones.

At His Feet

Romans 13:7

King James Version (KJV)

7Render therefore to all their dues: tribute to whom tribute is due;

custom to whom custom; fear to whom fear;

honour to whom honour.

I want to personally honor all the ones who had the greatest impact on my life during my time in jail. These Men and Women of Faith are true servants of the Kingdom. They do it for the Glory of God not for themselves! They walk in the greatest power on the universe: unconditional love.

I will never be able to repay these people for what they have done for me. However, I know they have great rewards from the Father awaiting them in Heaven and on Earth.

At His Feet

The first minister I will honor, Missy Webb,   Missy has been a

blessing to me and my church. She has ministered at Living Waters

Ministries (a church where I once was pastor with my husband) where she has

led several more broken people to Jesus Christ. She still preaches

with the same love and fire from God and will be a forever friend.

We have worked together in ministry, giving our testimony of how

God placed us together. I look forward to working with her in the

Kingdom for years to come.

At His Feet

Tammy Sheppard, has never left my side.

She is the closest friend I have ever had. We talk on a weekly basis and encourage one another. She has had the greatest impact on my life of anyone that God has placed in it thus far.

At His Feet

Chaplain Mark Miller showed me that you can have joy serving the Lord. I never saw this man without a big cheesy grin on his face. He taught about the Love of God and that God wanted us to enjoy life. Thanks, Mark, for helping me laugh in such a dark place.

Charlie Abraham has been the voice of God many times for both myself and Living Waters Ministries. Through my meeting Charlie God has blessed our entire county. Charlie has become a Spiritual Father to so many people in McDowell County, West Virginia and surrounding areas. God sent him to our church in order to spark the fires of revival in many churches throughout this region. Charlie walks in more love than anyone I have ever known. If I need him, he's always there. Thanks, Charlie!

Billy and Sabrina Manuel have been to Living Waters Ministries to share the love of God. I visit Billy's mother's church and minister about once a year to the ladies.

His mother and sister, Francis and Elizabeth Manuel, also had a huge impact on my life both inside and outside of jail. Now I feel as if the Manuel family is part of my family. I love them all very much.

At His Feet

Colleen Addair has become like a sister to me. She Ministers in worship at Living Waters ministries whenever I need her. Her anointed voice has destroyed many strongholds over McDowell County. She drives from Knoxville, Tennessee to McDowell County because of her love for the people here and her love for me. Most of all, it's because of her love for Jesus. Colleen is a native of this county and has a heart to see it restored.

Dana Stafford, Colleen's sister is also a huge support to me in the ministry. She has taught at the church and shown me the kind of woman I aspire to be. Full of Grace and full of the Word of God, this woman is a true inspiration.

At His Feet

Chaplain Morrow and I have recently regained contact with one another through phone conversations and email. I do hope to see him soon. His part in my life I know is not over.

So you see, never take the people God places in your life for granted. He knows who to place in your path and who to take out. He uses every part of your life and as you look back you can see how it all comes together like a beautiful masterpiece. Spend much time at His feet, get to know Him and let Him do in your life what you thought could never be done.

I know this is just the halfway point for me, God has many exciting adventures on my horizon. Some I will enjoy, others not so much. One thing I know for a fact: good or bad, I will always find myself worshipping **At His Feet.**